Refreshing
the Teacher's Soul

Compiled by Tim Wesemann

The mission of CTA is
to glorify God by providing purposeful products
that lift up and encourage the body of Christ!

because we love him.

www.CTAinc.com

Refreshing the Teacher's Soul

compiled by Tim Wesemann
www.timwesemann.com

Copyright © 2008 by CTA, Inc.
1625 Larkin Williams Rd.
Fenton, MO 63026

Unless otherwise indicated, all Scripture is taken from the HOLY BIBLE, NEW INTERNATIONAL VERSION®.
Copyright © 1973, 1978, 1984 International Bible Society. Used by permission of Zondervan. All rights
reserved.

Scripture quotations marked ESV are taken from The Holy Bible, English Standard Version, copyright ©
2001 by Crossway Bibles, a division of Good News Publishers. Used by permission. All rights reserved.

ISBN 978-1-933234-70-0
PRINTED IN THAILAND

To: _____

From: _____

*[The LORD] will rejoice over
you with gladness; he will
quiet you by his love.*
Zephaniah 3:17 ESV

Dear teacher,

No doubt you feel parched at times. Perhaps you search for clues that what you do makes a difference. Dehydrated, maybe you long to drink from the stream of grace flowing from the heart of your Teacher— the ultimate Teacher!

Be assured your Lord has a heart filled with compassion for you. What's more, he recognizes your passion to teach others about the heart of their Savior. He wants to refresh you with the Living Waters of his Word and rejuvenate you with his kindness as you hear the kind words of others.

I pray the words on the following pages will resonate in your life; reinforce your calling from God to teach his children; and provide inspiration, encouragement, and joy!

[The LORD] will rejoice over you with gladness;
he will quiet you by his love; he will exult over
you with loud singing.
Zephaniah 3:17 ESV

Lord,
you have refreshed my soul
with your presence and promises!
I celebrate my calling to teach
your children!
Amen.

I know my teacher really cares because . . .

. . . she looked each of us in the eye and said she loved us.

Lauren, age 9

. . . he cheered me on in my cross-country race, and he has spent his time making me smile.

Heather, age 11

. . . he helps us with a problem we do not get.

Caroline, grade 5

. . . she explains to us when we make a mistake, like what was wrong.

Abby, age 8

. . . she teaches us to pray.

Mary, age 6

No, Mommy, that's not my pretend friend.
It's Jesus. My teacher says he walks with us
wherever we go.

Paloma, age 6

Thank you for teaching me everything I know about
God. It is so good to know you care.

James, age 10

*Come to me, all you who are weary
and burdened, and I will give you rest.
Take my yoke upon you and learn from me,
for I am gentle and humble in heart,
and you will find rest for your souls.
For my yoke is easy and
my burden is light.*
Matthew 11:28–30

The best thing about being a teacher is . . .

. . . you get to do what you love—teaching.
Lauren, age 9

. . . you get to hang out with kids every day and guide and teach them.
Will, age 12

. . . eating popcorn on lunch break.
Austin B., age 6

. . . being loved by your students.
Briana, age 12

. . . you get free apples.
Ashley, age 8

. . . you get to teach about Jesus.
 Ryan, age 8 and
 Emily, age 10 1/2

. . . you don't just teach but learn.
 Micah, age 11

Therefore, as God's chosen people, holy and dearly loved, clothe yourselves with compassion, kindness, humility, gentleness and patience. Bear with each other and forgive whatever grievances you may have against one another. Forgive as the Lord forgave you. And over all these virtues put on love, which binds them all together in perfect unity. Let the peace of Christ rule in your hearts. . . . And be thankful. . . . Whatever you do, whether in word or deed, do it all in the name of the Lord Jesus, giving thanks to God the Father through him.
 Colossians 3:12–17

Why do you think Jesus picked your teacher to teach children about him?

She has all the skills and love.
Micah, 11

He knew she would talk about him everywhere.
Emily, age 9

She needed a good job.
Kyrie, age 8

He liked her as his child.
Ryan, age 8

She makes school fun.
Paige, age 9

He's a very good teacher. I would pick him!
Natalie, age 11

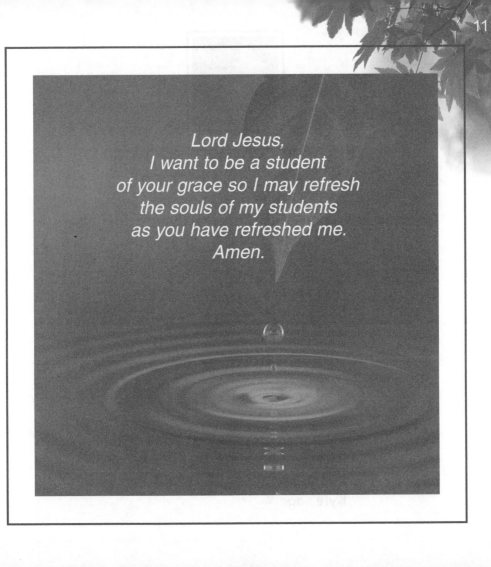

*Lord Jesus,
I want to be a student
of your grace so I may refresh
the souls of my students
as you have refreshed me.
Amen.*

What do teachers do when they're not teaching?

Go home and take a nap because they're tired.
Allie, age 5

More school work.
Cole, age 9

Do normal people stuff and grade papers.
Andrew, age 10

Go home and e-mail people.
Ashley, age 4

Don't talk.
Nathan, age 4

Just sit there, I think.
Kyle, age 4

Go to a meeting about being a good teacher.
>   Danny, age 5

Study about God.
>   Bailey, age 8

Get ready for Sunday school.
>   Rachel, age 10

Go to the teacher's lounge and drink soda.
>   Chris, age 9

Grade papers, and if they did something wrong ask God to forgive them.
>   Nicole, age 10

They're always teaching. Except for when it's time for lunch or recess.
>   Olivia, age 11

*I can do everything through
[Christ] who gives me strength.*
Philippians 4:13

My teacher loved each of us. She didn't "force" Jesus
on us, constantly telling us what to do and how to do
it. Instead, she let us know that she wasn't perfect—
she did things wrong, she made mistakes, and her faith
had been weak too. She first and foremost cared about
us and our lives, and we began to see where she was
coming from, which strengthened our faith, even
if we didn't know it at the time. Because she tried so
hard to connect to us without being overbearing and
pushy, we trusted our lives to her and were willing
to give the same amount back to her . . . and we
saw what she wanted was for us to trust in Jesus.
And so we did wholeheartedly.

Kirsten, age 17

A good teacher is someone who is not just good at math or something, but is also kind and helpful.

Madison, age 12

For we are God's workmanship,
created in Christ Jesus to do good works,
which God prepared in advance for us to do.

Ephesians 2:10

Thank you for the greatest two years of school I've ever had.

Robby, age 12

*Let us not become weary in doing good,
for at the proper time we will reap a harvest
if we do not give up. Therefore, as we have
opportunity, let us do good to all people,
especially to those who belong to the
family of believers.*

Galatians 6:9–10

Every year my teacher still sends me a Christmas card with a prayer written in it. I always get a card for special occasions—the birth of a child, major events. She played endless games of Clue when she babysat my sister and me. She doesn't even like the game, but we didn't know it.

K., mom of four

My teacher could almost cry because she loves Jesus so much.

Courtney, age 9

The best thing my Sunday school teacher taught me is that Jesus loves everyone no matter what.

Karissa, age 7

Now go; I will help you speak and will teach you what to say.

Exodus 4:12

What do teachers pray about?

Me. And anything else that they need help or strength or patience for. In childhood I had a teacher who told us she constantly remembered us in prayer, because she knew growing up was hard to do.

Stephanie

I think they pray about having great ideas for the big, upcoming math test.

Paula, age 9

Lord,
my students overwhelm me some days.
When I'm at the end of my rope, they
unexpectedly throw me a lifeline with a word or
even a look. Their insights help me refocus,
help me remember what's truly important.
Their unexpected comments can take me
from losing it to laughter. They look at situations
in ways I have never explored. When I'm taking
myself too seriously, their smiles can seriously
change my thinking. Thank you for those
moments. Thank you for my students.
Thank you for overwhelming me with your
love in their lives and your love in my life.
Overwhelmed with grace, I'm yours.
Amen.

Rejoice in the Lord always.
I will say it again: Rejoice!
Let your gentleness be evident to all.
The Lord is near. Do not be anxious about
anything, but in everything, by prayer and petition,
with thanksgiving, present your requests to God.
And the peace of God, which transcends all
understanding, will guard your hearts and
your minds in Christ Jesus.

Philippians 4:4–7

Thank you for teaching me all about God! I learned so much from you teaching us. You got me really pumped up every day for religion class. Thank you so much!

Olivia, age 11

What's the most important thing your teacher taught you about Jesus?

Well, I can remember it as clear as eating
a cookie. That Jesus died for me.
        Paula, age 9

That Jesus always, no matter what, loves you.
        Emily, age 13

That we all are sinners and that Jesus saved us from it.
        Jacob, age 9

That Jesus' love never ends.
        Keegan, age 8

That he loved me enough to die on the cross from my sins.
        Justin, age 12

So much I don't think that I can name it all!
        Trista, age 9

Excerpt from a letter a parent wrote
to her daughter's first-grade Sunday school
and Christian day school teachers:

I wanted to let you know that God is working through your words and actions and bringing about change—not just in my daughter Sarah, but in my life as well. One particularly hectic day, Sarah was in the backseat of our car while I drove down the interstate. Her seat belt was cinching too tightly around her waist, and it was uncomfortable. I told her she'd have to wait until the next exit so I could pull over and help.

"I wish that whole apple thing had never happened," Sarah complained from the backseat.

"What whole apple thing?" I asked.

"You know, Mom. Adam, Eve, the snake . . . the whole apple thing. If the whole apple thing hadn't happened we wouldn't even need seat belts, 'cause everyone would drive right," Sarah replied.

The rest of the trip we talked about whether we would even have cars, whether we'd need to go any-where, or need to go anywhere quickly if "the whole apple thing" had never happened. We talked about heaven and what it's like, about how God cares for us by giving us inventions like seat belts. The rest of my day took a different focus.

I know it was what she heard and talked about in school and Sunday school that helped her make the connection. I just thought you might like to know that even when you are talking to a class of wiggly first graders, God is using your words. Thank you for caring to serve my daughter.

Whatever you do, whether in word or deed,
do it all in the name of the Lord Jesus,
giving thanks to God the Father through him.
Colossians 3:17

My teacher loves Jesus so much that he shaved his head for kids with cancer.
Will, age 12

Good teachers do stuff good.
Danny, age 5

Thank you for teaching me what you teach me. I love that you do that.
Alexis, age 10

My teacher loves Jesus
so much that . . .

. . . she teaches us about all the wonderful things he
did for us.

Megan, age 9

. . . she cares for every student she had.

Robby, age 12

. . . she praises him in every prayer.

Mary, age 6

*O LORD, you are our Father. We are the clay, you
are the potter; we are all the work of your hand.*

Isaiah 64:8

The best thing about being a teacher is . . .

. . . you know all the answers to tests.
Karissa, age 7

. . . you get to be in charge, you get to write things up on the board, and you get to grade papers.
Brooke, age 10

. . . you get to see kids!
Jeff, age 9

. . . the power.
Nolan, age 8

. . . you get a big desk all to yourself.
Kyrie, age 9

. . . you get cake and stuff for the kids birthdays.
Sara, age 7

Dear Jesus,
I see so much when I look into the eyes
of the students you have called me to teach.
Wonder. Confusion. Strength. Hurt. Joy. Worry.
Curiosity. Uninhibited dreams. There's so much
going on behind those eyes! But my joy comes
when I see you in their eyes. I pray that my
students also see you when they look into my
eyes as we walk together in faith, always
learning about your Word and your world.
Amen.

What would you like your teacher to know you'll never forget about God?

That I love God and I always will!
> Emily, age 11

He'll never stop loving us.
> Mary, age 6

That I know I have eternal life.
> Brandon, age 12

He loves *all* of us.
> Zachary, age 12

Dear Teacher, thank you for being a great *roll* model for me.
> Ali, age 11

Thank you for being my teacher. I can tell you're a Christian.

        Mitchell, age 9

*Let us not love with words or tongue
but with actions and in truth.*
      1 John 3:18

*As the deer pants for streams of water,
so my soul pants for you, O God.*
      Psalm 42:1

How can you tell your teacher loves Jesus?

Because she told me.
                    Paloma, age 6

She has pictures all around with him on them.
                    Cole, age 9

He respects everybody else.
                    Will, age 12

She's my mom!
                    Micah, age 11

Because he incorporates Jesus into our math lesson.
Mason, age 12

She has a poster that says, "Jesus Is My Best Friend."
Ashley, age 8

She is nice and patient and very kind and understanding.
Alex, age 10

Because when she speaks of him she sounds happy.
Brennen, age 10

*God has poured out his love into our hearts by
the Holy Spirit, whom he has given us.*
Romans 5:5

*To him who is able to do immeasurably
more than all we ask or imagine, according
to his power that is at work within us, to him be
glory in the church and in Christ Jesus throughout
all generations, for ever and ever! Amen.*

Ephesians 3:20–21

When a teacher loves Jesus, she talks about him
a lot and smiles a lot too.

Jane, age 12

The most important thing my teachers have taught me
about Jesus is that he is our Savior, he died for us,
and he gives us eternal life so that someday we can
live with him in heaven.

Ali, age 11

Dear Teacher, thank you for *tiching* me to
be *smert*.

    Andrew, age 9

A good teacher is someone who helps you learn,
but also lets you learn things on your own.
            Mosie, age 11

My teacher knows what I need.
            Mary, age 6

Dear Teacher, thank you for helping me in my walk
with Christ, and thank you for educating me in the
way you have.
            Rachel, age 10

*How great is the love the Father has
lavished on us, that we should be called
children of God! And that is what we are!*

1 John 3:1

My teacher is sweet and she gave all of us seven hugs on our birthdays. And when my dog died, she sent me to the school counselor to talk about it. She shows me Jesus' love.

Eliott, age 7

My teacher tells us about Jesus every day.

Lauren, age 9

My teacher tells me that . . .

. . . God is full of truth.
       Nolan, age 8

. . . the Bible is God's Word.
       Paige, age 9

. . . God has sent his Son, Jesus, to die on a cross and rise from the dead to save all of the believers from sin, death, and the devil.
       CJ, grade 5

. . . if you believe in Jesus you will be saved.
       Lindsey, age 8

What do teachers pray about?

I think they pray. . .

. . . that they don't mess things up.
K.S., age 8

. . . that their sins could be washed away.
Sarah, age 8

. . . that their students don't get any louder.
Claire, age 10

. . . to help them get through all the bad stuff.
Ryan, age 8

. . . that they don't lose their jobs.
Sam, age 7

. . . for us to get good grades.
Eli, age 8

. . . about their students because they care about us
more than we can imagine.
Mackenzie, age 11 1/2

Refresh.
Revive.
Restore.
I love your lesson plans for my life, Jesus.
I have so much to learn from you
about teaching. Thank you for giving
me a place in your classroom.
Amen.

So then, just as you received Christ Jesus as Lord, continue to live in him, rooted and built up in him, strengthened in the faith as you were taught, and overflowing with thankfulness.

Colossians 2:6–7

My teacher likes to read different languages of the Bible, like Hawaiian.

Ryan, age 12

I think a teacher is a good teacher when you feel you can talk about anything with them.

Em, age 13

My teacher loves others as much as she loves herself.
Lindsey, age 8

Thank you, teacher, for caring about my life outside of school and for taking your time to talk with me.
E.R., age 13

[Jesus said,] "'Love the Lord your God with all your heart and with all your soul and with all your mind.' This is the first and greatest commandment. And the second is like it: 'Love your neighbor as yourself.'"
Matthew 22:37–39

*The joy of the L*ORD *is your strength.*
Nehemiah 8:10

After school, my teacher goes home and cooks dinner for his wife.

Chelsea, age 12

A good teacher gives us a lot of recesses and free time and gives us extra food and ice cream and doesn't give a lot of homework.

CJ, grade 5

Teachers get to teach little kids. The little kids teach the littler kids or babies. The babies teach the pets.

Megan, age 9

Thank you for everything that you do, and thank you for loving me and protecting me and doing whatever you can to teach me.

Michala, age 9

Teachers tell the most cheesy jokes ever.

Aaron, age 11

I thank my God every time I remember you. In all my prayers for all of you, I always pray with joy because of your partnership in the gospel from the first day until now, being confident of this, that he who began a good work in you will carry it on to completion until the day of Christ Jesus.

Philippians 1:3–6

What do teachers do when they're not teaching?

Grade papers, do word searches, and play spider solitaire.
Evan, age 9

I don't really know what teachers do when they're not teaching, maybe they watch *Dancing with the Stars*.
Brandy, age 12

They get ready for Sunday school.
Rachel, age 10

Well it's not like they don't have a life. They probably play sports, spend time with their family, and go out with friends.
Abbie, age 11

I think they party in the teachers' lounge-coffee room.
Van, age 11

*I have been crucified with Christ and
I no longer live, but Christ lives in me.*
Galatians 2:20

As an adult now, looking back, I hope my teacher
knows that one thing I'll never forget that she taught
me is that I am a redeemed, forgiven, dearly loved
child of God who is being changed daily and eternally,
and that God doesn't waste his love on me. He lavishes
his love on me, and I can be generous in loving other
people because he has been so generous to me.

Kenda

44

My teacher loves Jesus so much that . . .

. . . she sacrifices most of her time.
James, age 10

. . . she would give up her house for Jesus.
Andrew, age 10

. . . she would do anything for him.
Lauren, age 9

. . . she has a Bible.
Kyrie S., age 8

. . . he teaches wild kids about him.
Tory, age 10

I think that the best thing about being a teacher is watching the people you teach learn and understand how to do it.

> Mosie, age 11

I see teachers serving Jesus all the time by just plain teaching. But I don't think that's the beauty of teaching. I'm sure most people don't know of the connection my teacher made to me. She didn't go out of her way so that people could *see* her touching my life. She just did. And that's what makes a special teacher a special teacher.

> KLC, grade 11

Well done, good and faithful servant!
Matthew 25:21

Why do you think Jesus picked your teacher to teach children about him?

Because he has a plan for everybody.
William, age 11

God knows what's best for us.
Thomas, age 8

She is creative and thinks of new ways to give the lesson.
Jane, age 12

"For I know the plans I have for you," declares the LORD, "plans to prosper you and not to harm you, plans to give you hope and a future."
Jeremiah 29:11

I see my teacher serve Jesus when she sings her best using her best voice when we sing praises.

Zachary, age 8

The best part of being a teacher is having the feeling, "I am changing a life teaching these children."

Corie, age 11

I think the best part about being a teacher is being able to see students understand something for the first time.

Emily, age 13

Therefore . . . stand firm.
Let nothing move you.
Always give yourselves fully
to the work of the Lord,
because you know that your labor
in the Lord is not in vain.
1 Corinthians 15:58

Dear Teacher, thank you for loving me.
Sydney, age 10

If this book has made a difference in your life or if you have simply enjoyed it, we would like to hear from you. Your words will encourage us! You can reach us at:

Editorial Manager, Department RTS8HC
CTA, Inc.
PO Box 1205
Fenton, MO 63026-1205

or by e-mail at editor@CTAinc.com.
Please include the subject line: RTS8HC.